Star Gazing

Poems of Astronomy

by

Miriam Sagan

Cholla Needles Arts & Literary Library
Joshua Tree, CA

Dedicated with thanks and gratitude to my husband Richard Feldman who has shown me the sky and so many other things. – Miriam

Star Gazing

*Thanks to Art & Soul Residency
in Truth or Consequences,
New Mexico, where
this book was
completed.*

Part 1

footprints in snow
crescent moon, all my
beautiful failures

Ptolemy

we thought
we were the center
of the universe

we thought
we could fly
until our waxen wings

melted
in the heat
of the sun...

first week Freshman
at the great university
in the intro

to astronomy lecture
where they showed
earth as just a speck

in cold space
my sister began to weep
went to find

me—older,
an upperclassman
seeking reassurance

I'm homesick
for a notion
of the past

the centrality
of my version
of the story

spheres within spheres
for my tribal god
who arranged light

out of chaos
for my ancient
fixed self.

Who Put The Moon In The Driver's Seat?

driving with an obscured windshield
who put the moon behind the wheel?
who put the moon in charge of daylight?

a pregnant woman
should wear a key
or at least a big safety pin

during an eclipse
everything
turns

the moon comes to a complete stop
and makes a safe legal turn
as to that key

it is like the ones
the expelled Jews took out of Spain
that opened the gates of high walls

overgrown gardens
broken Moorish tiles
key to a lock

you can look right through
as if it were
a keyhole-shaped window

to see the moon.

Remedial Class at the Planetarium

Enjoys seeing "O'Ryans belt"
Didn't know there was a bear in the sky
Thinks the moon landing
Was a conspiracy
And thanks me because
They love astrology

The physicist says
My face in the mirror
Is nanoseconds younger
Than my real face
Because of how
Light travels
(memory asks
how did I get so old?)

And then one student says:
Where there is a lot of space
There is a lot of time...

Aspects of the Moon
after Yoshitoshi

in the moonlit
moments before
the first brushstroke
of Genji

the madwoman
unraveling her dead lover's letters
the student
reading by moonlight

the great general
headed towards his defeat
in a boat on the lake's
moonlight wake

moonlight
is the fourth string
on the three-stringed
instrument

pointing a finger at the moon
still showing off—
you think that answered
my question?

you used to call this
"the floaty life"
just hanging around
the old apartment

the first thing
I ever realized was beautiful
moon rising over the dunes
at Fox's Bottom beach

the moon
men walked on…
was it
THIS moon?

you didn't get up early
you stayed up
all night
moon

it repeats
diminishes
grows
maybe you were right after all

Nightsky

Antelope, jack rabbits, dusk
Comes on
Civil twilight, then nautical
As if light were a little ship
Slipping over the horizon
Sirius, Dog Star brightest at any latitude
Contrails like speedboat wake
Give way to velveteen sky
Saturn, whose rings we can't see
Without the binoculars
We left on the shelf at home,
Castor and Pollux
Shining on either side.
And gradually, like invisible ink
The constellations you point out
Begin to define themselves
Dipper, Orion,
The city of Albuquerque faint glow to the north.

Stars come out in nightsky, cryptobiotic
Mark direction
As clearly as in the planetarium.
Planes above us headed somewhere else
I'd like to know
Where
And how each passenger
Is doing, reading, dozing,
Worrying about the past
As ice clinks in plastic cups.

Try painting all this
With whiteout
On carbon paper.
On earth
The flying star weed called Datura.
I'm cold, now, ready
To go
You say—"you do the Cliff Notes
Of altered states."

Aldebaran, Betelgeuse, Procyon
And smoke from the Manzanos
Burning all night
Highway flashing sign
FIRE ACTIVITY AHEAD.

These stars
Like the ceiling
Of the Shaffer Hotel:
Lion's head, masked dancers,
Backwards swastikas of migration
Thunderbird, lightning zigzag,
A narrative of relocation.
These stars
By dawn
Will unfold their wings
And fly away again
Like mourning doves in the yard below us.

Augury

the air controller brings us down out of the cold sky
goes home to sleep behind a lit window,
she dreams the moon loses the earth's orbit

this is no iron age and yet
the metallic taste of war persists--
spirit campfires rake the north

I dreamed I was sleeping
in Iceland on a Tuesday
in January

looking into the dark earth
as if into a crystal pool
the dragon-prowed ship appeared in the mist

Pillar of Smoke by Day

stacked up over Greenland
aurora borealis
darting among clouds
like a pillar of fire by night
eye level with the plane

arriving in total blackness
sleet and
driving rain

I wanted to
enter
myself
again
but from a different
angle--
darkness.

Aurora Borealis

I went out seeking
the northern lights
on a tour bus
in Iceland
in the middle
of the Arctic night
found instead
hundreds of Chinese tourists
eating waffles with jam
drinking hot chocolate
from a machine

stood in a field of snow
beneath a brilliant then clouded moon
where words
that make me happy
like "rift" and "continent"
write a story

the whole time I was--
convinced? more like aware
of darkness as a figure
a person somehow
not personified
or a figure of speech
but simply someone standing there

back in Reykjavik
at 1 am
the street was hopping
Kiki's Queer Bar
shone rainbows from its disco ball
drunk handsome boys
tossed vodka soaked limes
into the air
and here, long-long-legged in fishnets
micro minis, sweeping hair
girls who party through the nights--
I think I saw the northern lights

Dark Country

lava flow
starts at the edge
of this white bed

twenty hours of night sky
filled with the glowing objects
of god, and man

moon sinking
after breakfast
power plant lit red green yellow red

uncurtained window--
what I fear,
face of a troll

not enough
daylight
to turn to stone

a wolf in a trap
my father
paralyzed by stroke

and the creamy pale
azure
of blue lagoon

floating in mist
hot water
reborn

moon comes up
again, long night
follows dawn

I go on
being all this
at once.

dream of the white bear,
the winds point the way—
lost prince's castle,
an embroidered sun
bone cold moon

winter's night,
a girl chained to a rock—
cold constellation;
falling stars illuminate
the fairy-tale book

hunters chased the bear
into the sky, blood dripping
turns the maples red
winter constellations rise
tonight in the old story

Eclipse of the Moon at Hotel St. Marie

you lean from the balcony
trying to see the moon

then make love to me
as if we had just met

by cold morning, through a window
you see the disc covered by darkness

like the slow street mimes
whose motion impresses as stasis

drip of a fountain
persists in the courtyard

mossy stone nude
half drapes herself

and the artificial pool
beneath green umbrellas and a palm tree

seems real.

Andromeda's Tears

Star birth—star death
Rings of Saturn—Jupiter's moons
Or Pluto seen as a double planet
You and I circling each other this entire lifetime.
I am a woman with two husbands
One dead, one living
Widow, wife, or a girl
Chained to a rock
Waiting for the dragon.
Certainly you must be the hero Perseus,
Who makes a living looking at things indirectly
Skinny and dark-haired, with a narrow face
Your secret is you don't care
About Medusa, that messy lady
With snakes for hair
Your secret is that you love me
Your secret is…
You didn't even know you had a secret.

My mother is a starry W in the sky
Cassiopeia, Queen of Ethiopia, vain, absent.
My secret is that as a child

I loved to pull leaves off bushes
Or shred the white strands of flowers
Called Andromeda's tears
And throw the hard blossoms across the yard
My secret is: I am not really
Chained to the rock
I am free to walk away at any moment.
I want to see what you can do to free me
You have a sword
And something dreadful in that bag
I want to see just how far I can travel
On the kiss of a living man
And ten thousand of a dead man.
Blue stars are born in clusters
A galaxy through the telescope
Might be a one-celled creature
In a drop of pond water
My tears are free of everything but griefs
What infects me is not contagious
I'm standing in the sky on this rock of stars
You can have me. Put out your hand.

Comet Hale-Bopp

Why is a comet directly over my house?
Why is my husband dead?
Why is a meteor bit of ice and dirt
Lighting up dawn and dusk
Like a peacock spreading his tail?
This comet looks like a cutout
Of luminous paper from my daughter's
Paste the stars on the ceiling kit.
Why can't I glow in the dark?
Why was I never beautiful?
Why have I had so many lovers?
Because I glow in the dark.

The world was created for my sake.
The rabbi suggests I try and live this way.
Comets were created for the comet hunter—
The woman who has discovered the most
Sits on her couch with an afghan, smiling.
There is no thrill like it! she says.
The Japanese comet hunter modestly says:
It is the comet, not I, who should get the credit.
Even the Jewish comet hunter is beaming
As if he had never heard of history.

What does the comet want me to do?
To spend all my money on new summer dresses,
Particularly blue ones with pink flowers.

Why is the oil in my car leaking?
Did I leave the kettle on?
Why are you dead?
Will I get tired of asking this question?
Why do I keep wishing?
Is the telephone for me?
Will my lover kiss me?
Will I get to eat all of the black jelly beans
Out of the mix?

Will I find a comet
In an otherwise blank sky of memory
And get to give this comet my last name
Which was probably changed at Ellis Island
As if I were the comet's husband
And it a conventional wife?
Have I ever
Actually seen anything happen?
Will I ever stop saying the words
"My dead husband"?
Has the statute of limitations expired
On being a widow?
Is the check in the envelope?
Will I get to see lava flow?
Will I see a glacier?
What's for dinner?
Do my cats think?
Out of what womb did this comet come?

Across The Solar System in Moab

The Sun in the middle of a basketball court, then Mercury in the nearby public library. Walk a block to Venus. We had trouble finding Earth, located near a bridge (Rich said if this were a science fiction movie or book we'd be court-martialed for missing Earth). Along the creek to a tunnel housing Mars. The Asteroid Belt noted but not marked, and for Jupiter start driving out of town to mile marker 124. Saturn is at marker 123 and then we took a detour to admire some petro-glyphs by the golf course.

Uranus is mile marker 121, and yes, the solar system is big enough that by now we've left the county to find Neptune at 118, and Pluto (down-graded to dwarf but still present) at marker 116. On our way to the Needles section of Canyon-lands we just keep going, technically now out of the solar system. Moab was lovely with forsythia and perfect light on the red cliffs and pancakes for breakfast.

Wonderful to be on canyon floor looking up at red monoliths while Island in the Sky looks down. We hike the potholes—depressions in rough rock that flood in rain bringing to life tiny tough shrimp and crustaceans whose eggs may wait for years. The universe is a big place (so is Four Corners)—and I am happy to see at the end of the day, a nice motel in Cortez, Colorado with a swimming pool.

at the edge of Jerome

copper mining town
turned tourist
all verticals
poplar trees by the abandoned
mansion
and red globes outside former bordellos
now selling lingerie and skull jewelry
a young woman
stands in the darkness
on the road's shoulder
and takes
a picture
of the full moon
on her cell phone and if you had
any question
about what direction
things rise in

now you know

The astrologer says

the moon
doesn't care
about being a mother

Pink hollyhocks
Japanese gate lit all night like an exit from a
dream
kimono hung on the wall
where is she
the woman who wore it wrapped—
maybe ash
it's white silk
with a pattern of pink and red
chrysanthemums
I'm sprawled half-naked on the bed,
old, and pleased with myself

The counter girl
has a tat
of a woman's back
naked in a bath
so often
the day just turns
away from me
as if wanting
to be touched on the shoulder

Two red chairs
hummingbird
came and went
so many things arrive
all at once
half-expected

The name of the little house
is Spring Moon
which I am not
I misremembered it as
New Moon
which in a way
I am—
in darkness

.

a warty gourd—
the planet Pluto—
magnified pollen

pink roses
turn silver at dusk—
Venus in the east

it startles us
an unexpected guest—
full moon

open cluster
of the Pleiades—
spring rain

      moonlight on snow crust
      dark trunks of trees
      New Year's dream

the moon cannot be called able-bodied nor can I

eclipse of the moon—
so much
left unsaid

birdsong in mist,
an old tale of revenge—
in the birch forest
even the greatest archer
can't hit the moon

Touching the Earth

warrior star
of the evening
obscured by clouds

in the hard-shelled
egg of this
darkness

night settles down
without joy
or even sorrow

for the past—
its failure
and regret

even chamisa and salt brush
speak of something—
kindness

wind picks up,
my only
company

as dawn spreads
over the neighborless
expanse

of land to sky
in one
gesture

Full Moon Ceremony

I drew a circle of my blood
I stood inside and made a vow
I said that I would never move
Until the animals appeared

I stood inside and made a vow
On the men with coyote heads
Until the animals appeared
Or the women with speckled wings

The men with coyote heads
All my ancient twisted karma
And the women with speckled wings
Born from beginningless greed, hate, and delusion

All my ancient twisted karma
For I was born in New Jersey
Born from beginningless greed, hate, and delusion
But I don't want to die in New Jersey

I was born in New Jersey
A bell came from the far-away
But I don't want to die in New Jersey
The hall as cold as another country

A bell came from the far-away
A clangor for the white-faced moon
The hall was as cold as another country
I bowed like a surfer thrown to the wave

A clangor for the white-faced moon
I can't stay here for I must go
Like a surfer thrown to the wave
Into the blue light of those rooms

I can't stay here for I must go
Into the blue light of the television
That casts a blue light through these rooms
Into the blue lights of desire

Into the blue light of the television
Is this what I meant to say?
Into the blue lights of desire
Into the blue light of the corn

Is this what I meant to say?
I said that I would never move
Into the blue light of the corn
I drew a circle of my blood.

Part 2

"hazy moon," you say
"quick, write a poem"—
it's gone

Star Midden

winter stars, pebbles in the arroyo
what do you gather in, hold

islands in the seas, the body
as an image of the cosmos

what do you gather in, hold
alaya–a storehouse of senses and seeds

as an image of the cosmos
a place marked and swiftly abandoned

alaya–a storehouse of senses and seeds
like an Anasazi stone granary

a place marked and swiftly abandoned
Pleiades are a wound in the constellation

an Anasazi stone granary
Sirius, Betelgeuse, Aldebaran

Pleiades are a wound in the constellation
of the starry, horned Bull

Sirius, Betelgeuse, Aldebaran
color is vibration made visible

the starry, horned Bull
is just a kiln of suns

color is vibration made visible
fused across empty space

is just a kiln of suns
crucible, calligraphic

fused across empty space
distance is distance from the self

crucible, calligraphic
what does it mean to be lost

distance is distance from the self
the map drawn in the dirt erased by wind

what does it mean to be lost
even the blind know the horizon

the map drawn in the dirt erased by wind
a shadow falls behind, as does the past

even the blind know the horizon
a cast of dried mud and raindrops

a shadow falls behind, as does the past
anthills, packrat middens

a cast of dried mud and raindrops
your words written in radium

anthills, packrat middens
architecture is narrative

your words written in radium
your words written in dust

architecture is narrative
the opening exhibition is Polaris

your words written in dust
a meaningful north star

the opening exhibition is Polaris
my souvenir of the Milky Way

an inner north star
or destination

my souvenir of the Milky Way
islands in the seas, the body

or destination–
winter stars, pebbles in the arroyo

Mid-August. Venus and Jupiter so close in the eastern sky, 5:45 am, a little early for me, just as the neighborhood starts to wake.

Viewing it with you as if a celestial show put on for our delight, like Stravinsky's "Nightingale" a few evenings ago at the opera—all chinoiserie, a boatman in a boat on a river of blue ribbon beneath stage moon.

two kids
in one sleeping bag—
Perseid shower

Serpent Mound

coils in green grassy embankment
holds in its mouth
  an egg
  a world
  us
maps on the earth
celestial comet, or constellation
draco, moonrise, solstice
equinoctial heartbeat
switchback
where light rises, throbs, stands still
like a knife to the heart of sacrifice.

effigy figure of a woman hoeing a snake,
the museum label reads "a legend"
might be
  metaphor
  narrative
  the truth

this is what
the shaman sees from the air—
twin mounds
the sun
the moon

thistles, clover, Queen Anne's lace
cicadas seventeen years underground
the dreaming nymphs emerge
bug-eyed and winged
and butterflies:
mourning cloak, sulphurs,
confusing cloudywing, pearl crescent, blues—
so many butterflies
you want to close your eyes
and dream of transformation

sacrifice of turquoise
blue veins of earth's pulse
lying open to the sky

ask for rain
peace
in a prayer

petitions without vowels

Peek-a-boo

Peek-a-boo, for the baby's laugh,
Milky Way glued together by a massive black hole

Pulling stars, dust, and everything inward
In the constellation of Sagittarius.

The baby was born under Pisces
On a chilly lunch hour

What a relief she can crawl so quickly
On her fat sturdy legs.

For a while you could hide something
And she'd forget about it

Now she has "Object Permanence"
Which is why we can believe in G-d

Or that our country is right, or seek revenge,
But also that I still love her

Even though I'm in a motel
In Socorro, New Mexico.

When she sees me she'll do a little dance
Stick out her tongue in greeting, her special thing.

I tell her secrets, to remember the word *freedom*
In the Richie Havens song,

And that the stellar megalopolis
Is pulsing, though we can't see it.

Carrion crows, Eurasian jays
And of course magpies

Also have object permanence
As to the black hole

It is we, not the galaxy,
That must imagine the invisible.

The Time It Takes To Reach Us

You say you don't
think about happiness
rather how many minutes
it takes sunlight
to arrive on earth

but this
must be
happiness
the pink roses
have never
bloomed this
profusely before

eight minutes
can be a long time
in labor
in the MRI
in the zendo
waiting
for someone
by the bronze statue
in the square

it's too long
for one kiss
or one thought
or standing in line
for pie

but it's quick
so quick
compared to a fossil
trilobite
or a star

the sunshine
looks fresh
outside my window

yet you say
this distance
worries you...

yellow chamisa, purple asters—
every year his yahrzeit

two jars of
refrigerator pickles—
small moon at dawn

Chaka Khan—
how many decades I've shimmied in pjs!

they're flirting again—
101 students on autumn equinox

for a moment
I felt all alone
in the world

Writer's Colony

such a long time ago
on the back steps
at the MacDowell dining hall
I sat
watching
big moon rise
over the October fields

a woman, about the age
I am now
stopped and asked me
"Are you working?"
and I hadn't known
that I was
until now.

paper screen
can't hide the full moon, cold
of the new year

no stars tonight—
the mist of the coast
at rice planting

Star Axis 1

We'd been hearing about it for years—a sculptor was building a monolithic pyramid out in the desert, behind Santa Rosa. It was a naked-eye observatory, focused on Polaris, the North Star. Like Smithson's Spiral Jetty or the Lightning Field out by Quemado, Star Axis was an earthwork— heroic, shamanic, a huge vision built not by pharaoh's minions but by a crew with bulldozers.

There was a tour and we set out to join it, meeting at the intersection of highway and dirt. We passed a WIDE LOAD, one of those fabricated houses on a flatbed that my husband seemed oddly fond of, perhaps because he loved transportation and was less enthusiastic about home owning.

I was a bit dubious—maybe we'd show up and no one else would. Maybe this would go on the list of things I'd missed seeing in my life (the cathedral in Milan because I was asleep in the van, the eclipse of the moon on an overcast night).

blue mosque at Akko
chained shut Friday afternoon
I passed on a bus
what crusaders called Acre
so many years ago

Star Axis 2

But the tour was here. So up a steep dirt road, barely clearing it in the Toyota. And then, literally in the middle of nowhere's scrub of juniper and pinon, a partially built pyramid and below it an enormous gateway of stone with a flight of stairs up the cliff.

Precession is the astronomical term that explains why the night sky looks different than it did a thousand years ago. The staircase of Star Axis, when finished, will let the observer walk through time, look at the sky from a specific step and see what Sappho saw, or Genghis Khan. Polaris is only our North Star for about two thousand years.

Everyone climbed up into a cool chamber to listen to sculptor Charles Ross speak about his work. My bad leg kept me below and I talked to the intern, a young woman my daughter's age, from Seoul. "Which side of the river?" I asked, and she was amazed I'd actually been there.

in the women's baths
I stared at them and they
at me—
our foreign bodies
so similar

Star Axis 3

Beautiful views in all directions. This landscape was once a sea. The sculptor came down and I had one question--about the three-legged black dog sprawled in the shade.

On the way home we saw another WIDE LOAD, a house on the move. My husband said no, he didn't like them, he actually feared them. Yet he seemed happy to be living in a time when we have a North Star.

the three-legged dog
lying in the shade
of the pyramid
with her nose on her black paws
is named Star.

Time is you and me
on the moving walkway

constellations fall from the airport ceiling
back onto the star map

a sundial sits like a dry fountain
in the middle of a maze of boxwood

is this your real story
the one you tell over and over

the one you tell strangers in bars
or to put yourself to sleep at night?

out in the desert
in the huge meteor crater

an ancient city
is carved in tuff and lava

this is where the narrative turns
where stage fright becomes architecture

where you may try one door, then another
in this house you built yourself.

Eclipse Of The Moon

As if it were a bonfire, or accident
Neighbors gather in the sidewalk
To watch the total eclipse
Of moon by earth shadow

White disc in and out off clouds
Shaped from a Chinese painting
Moon turning reddish, orange-yellow
The kind of color dogs howl at.

I wrap myself in a blanket
My daughter climbs on the car
You remember my black-haired mother
Singing "Total Eclipse"

When we were kids
Even though
It was just a partial eclipse
Of the moon, so long ago.

Penumbra, umbra like per-shadow,
Or penultimate words
The moon charts a course of darkness
Reliable in its change.

Waking many hours later
From lust or fear or the glass of red wine
Four in the morning the white full moon rides high
Above our bed

    That's when I realize
    I love you both—
    The living and the dead.

Very Large Array

There was a library before the world began:
In Babylon, astrologers read the sky
Undissolvable cuneiform, or
Papyrus scroll, buried in a jar
Sand sifting over a lost gospel.

Long line of radio telescopes
Along the Y-shaped track,
Pointing skyward.
The physicist tells me
We are all listening.

Very Large Array
On the Plains of San Augustin
Like Easter Island
Heads all pointed
Inland out of the Trades.
Facing a quadrant
Of the universe
Receiving what?

As if time were a book
You could read in
Could touch like braille.
The photographer says:
Sometimes the best
Picture
Is behind you.

At the speed of light
You could come back and simply stand up
Walk up the garden path
Irritated or surprised
By what had changed in your absence.

Listening to the universe
Pour in
And I hear
In Truth or Consequences, New Mexico
This mind that
Holds two things at once
Or nothing at all.

Locator
After Nancy Holt

pattern of stars
cast
inside the concrete tunnels

shadow of the sculpture
falls on the exact date
of your anniversary

location
is also about time
as is a telescope

you look
much younger
in the photograph

the poles shift
more frequently
than a lot of things

the novelty
of Polaris
as North Star

don't look directly at the sun
or drink
from the sculpture garden's fountains

steps, staircase
vanishing point
of the past

and she was weaving
a pattern of a star
over Chaco

like seeing one's own eyelashes
surveyor
incidental

we look
happy
in the photograph

Alignment

A childless woman builds a tunnel of suns
And spends the rest of her life
Photographing it

You ask yourself
What it is possible
To recover from

An array of potholes
One for each
Visible planet

Where a woman will crouch in labor
Display the umbilical cord
Of a king

Now full of water
Now dry

Full Circle

you fell from the sky
like a star in daytime
stone
ingot, meteor

were caught in a net
pinioned wings
and who was spotting you?
God, a pool of water, the abyss

or everyone on stage
the Georgian acrobats,
the Russian tumblers
hurtling in their great swing across empty space

Icarus, your dream
was neither of liftoff nor disaster
you did not expect the midwife or the undertaker
just uninterrupted flight

as for me, I woke up
in the middle of the night to the words:
oh terrible ghats of the river
release me from rebirth.

Pantoum for Hildegarde

A string is strung across the cosmos
Pluck it once, pluck it twice
And it reverberates
Like the rings of a ringed planet

Pluck it once, pluck it twice
Women's voices in the stone abbey
Like the rings of a ringed planet
Rising out of an enclosed garden

Women's voices in the stone abbey
Rise to hot stars blazing
Out of an enclosed garden
An interval of angels

Rise to hot stars blazing
Blue dwarves, red giants
An interval of angels
Without which no blade of grass grows

Blue dwarves, red giants
No green tendril uncurls
No blade of grass grows
Without this winged encouragement

No green tendril uncurls
No letter of the alphabet
Without this winged encouragement
No final or first breath

No letter of the alphabet
Without this string strung across the cosmos
No final or first breath
Reverberates.

We Are Here

We wanted to see
the model solar system
in Door County, Wisconsin,
but couldn't find it.
Then came upon it unexpectedly
en route to the Coast Guard Station and canal.
The analemmatic sundial—
constructed on an ellipse—
needed a pointer. Turns out
my husband Rich made a good gnomon.
Casting a shadow
we discovered it was still August,
which it had been all month.
Rich got stung twice
by a yellow jacket
before he even reached Mercury,
but survived with a little tender
first aid care from me.

Keflavik

The satellite dish
In Iceland
Tracks sputnik
And my childhood
Hiding under the desk
From Russian bombs
Tracks dream
Tracks the inner fire
Of planets and the coldness
Of asteroids

The abandoned army base
With its bulbous tower striped white and red
Domes, geodesic structures,
Its tanks with haunting moonshell staircases
Seagulls perched on streetlamps
Barracks now full of students
Jets taking skyward
And everywhere the smell of the sea...

Tracks departure
Tracks my dead grandparents
Spooning borscht
Tracks how Russian
The Russian Jews still are
As packed and dressed
I must return and sit for a moment
In the apartment by the lake
So I'll return
To Iceland

Tracks muffled oars
Mist
New found land
Earth's satellite
The moon
I haven't seen emerge
Even once
In a month of these white nights...

the full moon
rises like a whole note
on the staff
of telephone wires . . .
you burst into song

five planets glow
once
in my lifetime
above even this
shabby neighborhood

crescent moon
over the border patrol,
winter solstice

looming range,
an abandoned water tank—
the passerby

waning moon—
the smuggler's charms
tied to a backpack

Miriam Sagan

Part 3

Venus over salt flats
three million acres
of bombing range

Cosmos

"Am I related to this guy
Carl Sagan, and who is he?"
My daughter wants to know.

Yes, I say, a famous—very
famous astronomer, and I think
he is your second cousin, once removed

because he was my father's
second cousin (my grandfather
was his great uncle)

or so we'd been told. Like many things
he was forbidden to us.
My father the atheist

kept a kind of kosher—
Carl Jung, no
Karl Marx, yes

Freud, yes
Lenin, maybe
at least he once told me

"the end justifies the means"
but I was a child, and helpless,
and I knew he was lying.

And for some reason
Carl Sagan, no
although his mother

had been an union organizer
and my grandfather
a factory owner

but somehow
we weren't
rooting for her.

When my brother was in grade school
he wrote our Carl, asking
"send me pictures of Venus"

for a school report
and miraculously
a large manila envelope

appeared
full of brilliantly colored, high-resolution
planets...

On his deathbed, Carl
told my first cousin
"You aren't really Sagans"

something about Ellis Island
and a brother-in-law's last name
"The Sagans are the smart ones."

Who could quarrel
with that assessment?
The famous astronomer

handsome and troublesome
like my father
made the last name

that isn't really ours
so well known
that at the cash register

people still ask me
and say
"billions and billions"

and I always laugh
and say "yes"
and "stars."

Yerkes Observatory

is closed, feels abandoned
as we walk along the green
lawn, still mowed,
and the encroaching trees

its refracting telescope
the largest in the world,
now, as this is still a rich country
it isn't yet a ruin

you need a lens
to see
and also
vision

you were here before, Wisconsin,
a camping trip
with people I never knew
you barely remember

I snap the camera
take the same picture
of the elegant dome
twice

as if looking for something
a future we can't see
even as the lake rises
and begins to lap at our shoes

Comet

A comet above my house
I wear a dead man's coat
I can't see the comet for the haze
Clouds, snow, a waxing moon.

I wear a dead man's coat
A Chinese merchant's of finest wool
Clouds, snow, a waxing moon
The night we said farewell

A Chinese merchant's coat of finest wool
Or the poncho you gave me second-hand
The night we said farewell
For the first time, or the last time

The poncho you gave me second-hand
Wraps around me like a lover
For the first time, or the last time
I watch a movie about astronauts

Wrap around me like a lover
Men in a capsule hurtle towards earth
In a movie about astronauts
I'm crying about something else

Men in a capsule hurtle towards earth
This comet appears once a lifetime
I'm crying about something else
Everyone else has seen it

This comet appears once a lifetime
Above my laundry frozen on the line
Everyone else has seen it
Rising in the quadrant of Arcturus

Beneath my laundry frozen on the line
You say I have a presence
Rising in the quadrant of Arcturus
And the dead I can't speak to

You say: "The comet is a presence"
I can't see for the haze
And the dead I can't speak to
Blaze above my house.

The Astronomer's Wife

I wrote a poem
with this title
when I was eighteen

and looking through a telescope
on the Cambridge Common
not by myself

but with some guy or other.
I was auditioning
the entire city

geology, coastlines,
God, English literature,
and the solar system

to see who, or what
wanted to be
my boyfriend.

I really don't think
I thought
I could love

this boy, barely a man
who adjusted
the eyepiece

so I could see
Saturn—looking like Saturn!—
pure and close

unobscured by fog
or the noxious mist
from the river.

Why didn't I think
I could be the astronomer?
After all, feminism

had already been invented
if not by me.
I hadn't

invented anything—
not a style of kissing
not even myself

not yet.

at the blue hour

I'm north of Taos
but see an imagined city where
the Egyptologist
inside a perfume bottle
watches the geometries
of space
the night sky
mapped
inside a tomb,
to sit in Paris or London
at dusk
and puzzle
over hieroglyphs
when others
drink
something intoxicating
from a glass
among the bustle
of a great city—
the homeless man
wrapped in layers
like a corpse
turned mummy of a king
lies on the curb
we pass by—
no one
even the pharaoh's
astronomers
really wants to see
the future—

in the photograph
the nude has turned
cobalt
like a cure
for something—
even if I
scry
into a pool of water
I might not see
Giza,

just Lama Mountain.

in taos they may say

listen to your body
as if it weren't
crying with a thirst
for god,
in the dead of night
stars
were too brilliant
streaking across
darkness
streaming down
over the basin land
the far-off range,
a blinking red light
looked as if a great
ocean liner
was plowing waves
before me,
I went back to bed
before I could get caught
watching the stars dance
like princesses
in a fairy tale

anyone should feel free
to say
they'll pray for me,
after all
Lama Mountain sits cross-legged
palms pressed together

my husband shows me Scorpius

with its fiery stinging tail
rising by the moon
beneath Jupiter
and the Summer Triangle
and the Dipper,
across the field
the campers chorus hallelujah
and two kids run off like mad
into the darkness,
if it weren't for you, I tell him,
I wouldn't know the names of the stars
if it weren't for me
you wouldn't know the story
of the shepherd
and the weaving princess stars
separated by the Milky Way
for all but one night a year,
for us to meet
you just have to take
522 north
and I'll be home
by Sunday,
but if we weren't
apart
I wouldn't know

Lama Mountain.

Observatory

Through the telescope
Saturn's rings
made me gasp aloud

the old guy
helping me up the stepladder
seemed gratified

as are all men
by the sound
of pleasure.

Vega was blazing
blue
as star sapphire.

Among bent and
anthropomorphic
Joshua trees

we picked up
a frazzled, pretty
hitchhiker

who, half sobbing, said
"I got lost
photographing the desert

and I lost
my boyfriend."
We dropped her at the campground

where day after day
water wears
boulders away

to the shapes
one sees
on mescaline

the moon
had been up all night
and like a frazzled housewife

still in her nightie at noon
was just thinking
of lying back down.

It's good we saw those rings
of ice and dust
I hear that in some million years

they'll melt, and will be gone.
Wind slapped my face
at the long view

and the moon
slipped into an unmade bed
and was done.

I'll always want
turquoise earrings, a bit
of sky

Saturn Returns, Old Thing

a tide came in not of water but of sleep

it was possible to break the line in more than one
way

the red numerals of the digital clock referred to
Sumer and Babylon

the story you walked into had already happened

so much sadness at the edge of the old
apartment

some moon wandering somewhere needs you

suns fell into this house and my bungalow slipped
into a pool of stars

assisted living—
no one
looks at the moon

the unemployed
across-the-street
neighbor
sits on the porch,
my father
in the stroke hospital
2,000 miles
to the east
and this unending
loneliness
of human life,
the west blazing out,
November dusk

Crepuscular

dusk, dawn
the Arctic sun
sits like a scrawny monk
on a fat cushion

facing the wall
seeking
by sitting still
neat trick if it works

but what is
hidden in plain sight
can't be got
or lost or found

so go out
take the coat
from its hook
go begging for daylight

After Image

dawn
over the great basin

turns earth colors
canyon striation: dark pink, pale red, orange

which burns to furnace
in my eye

accidental
retinal image

of explosion
floating

across eyelid
or blank page

as if I'd seen
something

I should never have
looked at directly

A Lockless Key
after a Massimo Bartolini installation, 1997

Some things are beautiful
With the life leeched out—
Atlantic tideline of moonshells,
Shark cartilage, those black
Egg sacs of skates
That until puberty I thought
Were four-legged
Headless sea creatures in their own right
Odd collections of paperbacks
Warping in the sea air
Pages buckling like fault-lines
A life spent in rented houses
Houses with two white chipped teacups
In each cupboard
Piles of children's games
Missing all the dice
Nests of mice beneath sofa cushions.
And the ring of keys
Each with its forgotten use
The missing lock
To somewhere else.

I once saw a houseguest
A beautiful woman with six months left to live
Read French Vogue
At the time I thought it
A poor choice—
Now I understand.

The yellow wall recedes from my touch.
At first I didn't see
The one-holed constellation in the roof
One star alone can make no pattern—
Bear, girl chained to a rock, queen, or lion.
Last night I wasn't exactly pleased
To see you run after the city bus in the dream
It must have been San Francisco
Because you were so young in your long beard
You banged on the window
Said *I just want to give you a hug before I die.*
I had a motto *Never write about your dreams.*
Dreams are a different
Kind of condensed milk in a red and silver can
That should only be drunk in black coffee
In the dark.

Only now do I notice stars shining
On the yellow kitchen table
Moving from the southern hemisphere
Into something unrecognizable.

My own shoes frighten me
Ordinary household appliances are marked
As we are—by the course of stars.
The burns on the breakfast toast
Are simply stars
Not yet born.

grown, beautiful
the child I bore beneath
the moon's eclipse

so empty–
pale sky
without cranes

cumulus sky
I peer blankly at
my dim acquaintance

Two Gray Hills rug
Hangs on the wall
Orion's belt
Hangs vertical in the sky
Winter solstice

Joshua Tree
twisting, half moon in the blue
daytime sky—
I limp along
on my bad hip

Space Port

verticality of poplars
water tank on the hill
I wake neither sad not happy

you can reach space
from Truth or Consequences, New Mexico
supposedly now

just by paying
what my father called
the Yankee dollar

or, you could
do as little
as possible

the way I do
drink coffee, cream and sugar
the New York regular

of my childhood
once, I was in Japan
once, I was in your arms

once, in Florence, Italy
but I didn't
appreciate it then

up behind the dam
scrub country
big empty buses

rattlesnakes foreclosure
you can say "archeology"
or "potable"

you can say
other worlds shine
in the firmament

not ours, though, these worlds
not even
this one

spring wind
in the apricot blossoms—
late afternoon
at the homeless shelter, men
watch a movie about astronauts

moon with a slit wrist
an exit visa
I wish that you
among all the dead
remembered me.

winter constricts
stars fall
into the bath tub

Pluto in Riverside

The scale model of the solar system
Spreads across greater Boston
Starts with the sun in the Museum of Science
Mercury in the lobby
Venus on the top floor of the parking garage
Earth outside the Royal Sonesta Hotel
Mars in Lechmere's Galeria
Where patrons might sip a cappuccino
Jupiter at South Station where the trains depart
With the romantic expectation of arrival
Saturn in the Cambridge Public Library
With Uranus in the branch in Jamaica Plain
And Neptune—across traffic and congestion—
Rests in a mall in Saugus.

We don't really have the time
To spend all day crossing city
And crowded suburb
And not in all this rain.
Still, I wanted to see at least one—
Pluto is in Riverside, not that far
From where we're staying—
The smallest, furthest planet
At the end of the line.

We start at the diner in Waltham
Over eggs and middle-aged conversation
With your old friends, coffee, home fries
Our parents, our children's lives
Somehow eclipsing our own
As if our goal were just to survive
And hold up our portion of the human race
Although a different look might cross a face—
Flirtation, memory of romance or anticipation
There's life in us yet, for God's sake.
The moment passes, pass the ketchup, salt
The economy is tanked, the government...
And do we really know?
And should we stay or go?

We pay the bill, it's freezing
Everyone agrees,
Sure, we'll go see Pluto
In the station, at the end of the trolley line.
It's free, and tiny, this side of the turnstile
I'm disappointed, I'd expected... what?
Something bigger than my thumbnail
A potato-shaped asteroid of a planet
Or maybe its moon, Charon
Or some vision
Of its atmosphere at perihelion
A trans-Neptunian object
Hard to see with an amateur telescope.
There is no tenth planet.

Pluto is named for Hades, king of the dead.
As a kid, I liked that story
Demeter and Persephone
The daughter out picking flowers
Long skirt, long hair, picking anemones
Petaled purple and red.
Then Hades breaks through the crust of the earth
On his black horse, and carries her down
Into the underworld.
At thirteen, I wanted to be snatched
Longing for someone bad to come along
Grab me out of my mother's white-shingled house
Where she'd yell *11:30! Don't forget your curfew!*
Down to Hell I'd go
Amethyst cave, the dead with coins on their eyes
Where blind fish swim thru the drip of limestone
Hades, bad boyfriend, I just knew he was coming.
I put my ear to the earth and urged him on.

Half a lifetime later
I dream of my mother's city, this Boston
Its subway lines and trolley
Where I stand on a platform in a vast space
And when the train pulls in I rush to ask
The dark gentleman in the three-piece suit
"Is this train in or out bound?"
And he answers, before the doors swish shut
And the train drops underground
"Everything here is inbound."

I can't read my own handwriting—hazy moon

Old Story

the moon
wanted the woman
he'd seen among reindeer

she wasn't beneath the wooden bed
or hidden under
the eyedazzler rug

she had turned
into a lamp
shedding heat and light

the moon bent down
to enter the low doorway
of the yurt

he was
sweating
like a suitor

she turned back
into a woman
with two breasts

the moon
said he would tell her
his twelve secret names

which together
make a year
of time

but in the morning
all she could
remember

was moon
moon moon moon moon moon
moon moon moon moon moon

moon

Part 4

parking tickets—
a star map in the glove
compartment

Total Eclipse

1.

pink geraniums
after the storm
waning moon

you say a total eclipse
of the sun
can be nicely seen

through a kitchen colander
I've run out
of the exact shade

of pink embroidery thread
for my cross-stitch
and can't match it

you say
we are going to drive to Nebraska
to see total darkness

2.

dropped stitch
purl two
forgetting to cross
the X on the cross stitch

what I neglected to say:
be safe,
I love you,
come back

the moon promises
she'll do it right
this time
go the whole way

and cover the sun's face
totally in darkness
so we won't have driven
across hundreds of miles

of yellow sunflowers
for nothing

3.

obelisk of the war dead
at the visitor's center
names gold
on black polished stone

I drink the too bitter
bottom-of-the pot
coffee
in a styrofoam cup

4.

god of
two horizons...
solar bark—
the boat of millions of years—

small oars or one red sail
you can propel yourself
across
and in the underworld of sleep

you can visit
all the shadows
of your different selves
aging king with golden flesh, silver bones,

and hair of lapis lazuli
even in this open
range country
men are cattle of Ra

5.

astronomers call the eclipse
a cosmic coincidence
how our satellite
can blot out the star of our sun

I've held my thumb up
to cover many things
I didn't want
to see

is it coincidence
I hold you in my arms
in this bed
held you long ago

and always will?

6.

a sculpted horse
of metal, more like a skeleton
than flesh but alive

and kind and sweet—
I pat it and add
encouraging words

next in the dream
an ancient white-haired woman
sits glowing

without hands
in a room
too bright

to look at directly
an Etruscan goddess
of dawn

engraved on the back
of the handheld mirror
and what is reflected

in the dustless
surface?
my gaze...

7.

there is no
blessing
for an eclipse
in Hebrew

although there are blessings
for a large crowd
first blossoms
a comet

putting on new clothes
earthquake
the passage of time
a rainbow

8.

through welding goggles
at a rest stop in Wyoming
on the edge of short grass
in a month named for a Caesar
or shadowed
through a kitchen colander
you have dragged all this distance
moon's shadow
creeps across the sun
dozens of tiny eclipses
projected like shadow puppets
set up on the back of a truck
in a village at dusk
somewhere in Central Asia

like all places
far from the sea
we look
for our heroic saga
in the sky
across a landmass
so enormous
it might contain even
our longing.

9.

you turn away from the sun
to count the cars
on the freight train

we've been
counting
for days

something observable
moving—like buddha nature—
across the northern plains.

10.

eclipse
drawn on a napkin—
Nebraska

11.

the waitress seems confused
about the cosmos
she says she was up on the roof
with her boyfriend
and did not see the eclipse
but then describes
how everything went dark
and a star hung in the sky
except her boyfriend
said it wasn't a star
it was... uh, a planet?

we feel confused
because this restaurant
indeed was in the path
of totality
and what else
could she have seen
although it makes me sad
that this single mom
doesn't know the morning star
the evening star
is the goddess of love.

12.

we're alone again in the car
driving through basin land
and not, viejo, getting any younger

in the dazzling light
of late afternoon—
east of the sun and west of the moon.

Sunspot

We stayed in an odd motel
incense from the altar
behind the front desk
permeated even our room
offering to a Hindu god
I don't remember
which one.

In the morning
snow had fallen and outlined
a group of metal sculptures
for sale along the side of the road
horses running
giant pots
waiting for an arrangement of something.

We drove up
the mountain
to the sunspot observatory
which looks indirectly
in cast shadow
at our
star.

That was one
of the warnings
of my childhood
to never
look directly at the sun
to not drink
out of decorative fountains.

To not ask
to not tell.
My daughter was young enough
to love the snow
on sculpted horses
to love the scent—
of attar of roses

rising in front of
a blue
multi-limbed god
perhaps not care that much
about the telescope
that follows the sun
as do we.

Mercury: The Bath House

I stretched out my old legs
my very old toes
in the concrete tub
where hot water
gushes from the earth
just for my aches and pains

all nine planets
were present at my birth
are present now
just not visible
today in January
in Truth or Consequences, New Mexico

the woman tourist said it was ugly here
little falling down town
with its decrepit charm
nothing prettier
than a string of Christmas lights
in the dusk

don't get me
wrong, I also
don't welcome
the messenger
between the living
and the dead

an email
I sent myself
appears years later
or roses
delivered
to the wrong address

I'd rather forget
than remember
in sleep
still, through the steam
of the bath
the rainy streets

of the metropolis I was born in
appear slick and reflecting
colored lights of the past.

Venus: The Warrior

feathered warrior with a spear
sometimes rising
sometimes in the underworld
playing hardball
on a keyhole-shaped court
playing jai alai
with a skull

or hummingbird
tiny and ferocious
sharp-billed
indomitable
even the little quail
scurrying beneath
palo verde

wear their headdresses
one black feather
swaying
from a helmet
which was the real
planet Venus?
morning star

evening star
brightest after the moon
casting shadows
or what we don't see
veiled by reflective clouds
of sulphuric acid
water there

once

Mars: Survivors

They play chess,
the chief of police
of the Balkan town
his Jewish friend

one night the policeman
appears with train tickets
for everyone in the family
he says:

my friend
I've been watching, and now
it's time for you to go
to live to tell the tale

I hear stories of war
of a mother and daughter
hidden in plain sight
on the streets of Paris

of a stranger
who puts a desperate family
in a taxi and sends them two days away
to Constantinople

I see Mars almost twinkling
in our atmosphere
flashing red
the color itself that

of spectrum
shifting away from us
the color
of other things

as well.

Jupiter: Patriarchy

every bad card
from the pack
turns up

The Emperor, the Devil
those fixed things
that refuse to change

who turned me
into an old woman?
time

when I was just
messing around, not
paying attention

it's never too early, or late,
to learn to say:
fuck with me, you die

to break a hold
smash
an instep

to survive
a mosh pit
and an unknown future

the largest planet
is ringed by moons
is bright, magnetic, heavy

The Great Red Spot
is a storm
that keeps raging

if you meet a guru
call it a day
don't follow

star or wanderer
do look at your feet
can you run in those shoes?

Saturn: Old Age

Joshua Trees
we sleep
beneath the rings of Saturn

Uranus: Emanation

The astronomer regards Uranus
from the city of Bath
where those cool holding pools
lap against ancient mosaic

you think of the past
as what?
a kind of perfection
a kind of disaster

either a colonnade in white marble
or the blood
that's washed away in time
unfinished

labyrinth
what's invisible
in the daylight
sky

you wanted continuity
about the difference
between yourself
and a maze

clutching the right-hand way
then the left
featureless at first
glance—ice, rock

then illuminated

Neptune: *Gates of Ivory and Horn*

In the dream she tells me
the dead can communicate with us.
I don't believe that, say, no

it is just as if the elevator
opened at the wrong floor.
You always say that, she says.

But when I wake up
I realize
I never say that

am not even sure
exactly
what it means.

The planet Neptune
can't be seen
with the naked eye

Its existence
is predicted
by a wobble.

Galileo thought it a fixed star,
and therefore isn't credited
with its discovery.

This doesn't seem quite fair to me.
It's an ice giant, and depending
on what you believe

the outermost planet
or second farthest
away from us.

You yourself
can compare this
to whatever pleases you—

the living, the dead.
Frankly I'm getting
a little worn out

comparing things all day
and then
in my dreams.

Don't forget, though,
metaphor works both ways
if sleep is its own expanse

of universe
then the cosmos
must also be sleeping—

sleepy, maybe
and having trouble
staying up late,

like me,
but asleep?
I think not.

Pluto: Ambivalence

we almost got hit
and killed
last night

on the road behind the dam
when another car
came out of nowhere

or—it's good
I hadn't pulled
into the lane

when the driver
took the turn too fast
or, luck saved me,

or a guardian angel
so I could
arrive on time

go to the party
with people not really
my friends

or...

you've been dead
almost twenty-five years
and I hear

a phone ringing
in a casita
without a phone

the music of the spheres
dazzles
over the rented house

mathematics implies a planet
the astronomer finds it
only smaller than imagined

America wants to discover
its own celestial body—and suddenly
there is Pluto over Flagstaff, Arizona

things come and go—
grief, amusement,
and the planet Pluto

I've changed my mind
and everything
and nothing

patterns arranged
to receive and delight
me—

and all those other
half-born
worlds.

Horoscope

tiny planets fell into the flower pot

the house I was born in appeared in my dreams

the astrologer said my chart showed sensuality—
then kissed me

the caller was anonymous
but I was expecting the ant guy

it was raining inside the house

tiny planets rose on my fingernails

the guy was to get rid of ants, not deliver them

it was snowing in the house
of money, coffee, and grief

the palm reader said I had a vitamin deficiency

my father said I'd never get into a good college

tiny planets fell like raw sugar
into my orange pekoe tea

my friends crossed from the house of
reminiscence into the house of regret

ants carried away the tiny planets

and brought one perfect turquoise bead
to the surface of the earth

Acknowledgements:

Some of these poems first appeared in the following books and chapbooks:

True Body, Parallax Press
The Widow's Coat, Ahshata Press
Map of the Lost, University of New Mexico Press
Tanka from the Edge, Modern English Tanka Press
Seven Places in America, Sherman Asher
Swimming in Reykjavik (e-book), Moon Publishing
The Electric Palm Tree, Flutter Press
Geographic, A Memoir, Casa de Snapdragon Press
Lama Mountain, Red Bird Press
Ikisan Station, Flutter Press
Luminosity, Duck Lake Books
Old Lady Haiku (e-chapbook), Title IX Press

In addition. poems appeared in these litmags:
*Cholla Needles, Gnashing Teeth, Modern Haibun &
Tanka Prose,* and *Viscaria Magazine*

Serpent Mound was part of a gallery show and
anthology at 516 Gallery, Albuquerque.
Star Midden was text for a collaborative
sculptural project at The Land/An Art Site,
Mountainair, New Mexico and The Land/A Gallery
in Albuquerque, New Mexico.
Time Is You and Me was written as poet of the
month for the Center for Contemporary Arts in
Santa Fe, New Mexico.
Pantoum for Hildegarde was written and
performed with a harp duo at First Presbyterian
Church in Santa Fe, New Mexico.

Other books by Miriam Sagan:

Dangerous Body (1976)
Vision's Edge (1978)
Talking You Down (1983)
Aegean Doorway (1984)
Dharmakaya (1986)
Acequia Madre: Through the Mother Ditch (1988)
The Paths from the Nudist Beach (1989)
Coastal Lives (1991)
True Body (1991)
Pocahontas Discovers America (1993)
The Art of Love (1994)
Dirty Laundry (1997)
Unbroken Line (1999)
Archeology Of Desire (2001)
Searching For A Mustard Seed (2003)
Rag Trade (2004)
Gossip (2007)
Map Of The Lost (2008)
Tanka From The Edge (2009)
Love & Death (2011)
Seven Places in America (2012)
All My Beautiful Failures (2013)
Geographic (2016)
Luminosty (2019)
Bluebeard's Castle (2019)
A Hundred Cups Of Coffee (2019)
Beasts (2020)

Miriam Sagan is the author of over thirty books of poetry, fiction, and memoir. Her most recent include *Bluebeard's Castle* (Red Mountain, 2019) and *A Hundred Cups of Coffee* (Tres Chicas, 2019).

Miriam is a two-time winner of the New Mexico-Arizona Book Awards as well as a recipient of the City of Santa Fe Mayor's Award for Excellence in the Arts and a New Mexico Literary Arts Gratitude Award.

Miriam has been a writer in residence in four national parks, Yaddo, MacDowell, Gullkistan in Iceland, Kura Studio in Japan, and a dozen more remote and interesting places. She works with text and sculptural installation as part of the creative team Maternal Mitochondria in venues ranging from RV Parks to galleries. She founded and directed the creative writing program at Santa Fe Community College until her retirement. Her poetry was set to music for the Santa Fe Women's Chorus, incised on stoneware for a haiku pathway, and projected as video inside an abandoned grain silo in rural Itoshima. Her blog is Miriam's Well - http://miriamswell.wordpress.com